Bob Chilcott

5 songs for upper voices

MUSIC DEPARTMENT

OXFORD
UNIVERSITY PRESS

OXFORD
UNIVERSITY PRESS

Great Clarendon Street, Oxford OX2 6DP, England
198 Madison Avenue, New York, NY 10016, USA

Oxford University Press is a department of the University of Oxford.
It furthers the University's aim of excellence in research, scholarship,
and education by publishing worldwide

Oxford is a registered trade mark of Oxford University Press
in the UK and in certain other countries

12

ISBN 978-0-19-335920-8

Music origination by Enigma Music Production Services, Amersham, Bucks.
Printed in Great Britain on acid-free paper by
Halstan & Co. Ltd., Amersham, Bucks.

Contents

Composer's notes

All for Love of One: My intention with this piece was to write a real singing melody to reflect the passion and beauty of this fifteenth-century text. It is designed as a two-part piece, but can equally be performed in unison by singing the melody at bar 24 in the soprano part and at bars 31 and 55 in the alto part.

The Truth is Great: I wrote this piece for a festival in Denver, the theme of which was nature and the environment. The lyrics reflect on how small we are in the great scheme of things. To me the sentiment is not earnest but wistful, with a touch of gentle humour. This piece can also be performed as a unison song by omitting the alto part.

Circles of Motion: This poem, by the living native-American poet Joy Harjo, has a wonderful strength and an affirming message, again reflecting on the inevitable circle of life. I imagine this song being sung with verve and a sense of empowerment.

All things pass: I love the profound yet simple wisdom in this poem, which, as in the lyrics of the previous two songs, suggests that ultimately we have very little control over our destiny. I find this kind of sentiment very strengthening and comforting, so have written music that will hopefully inspire positive and empowered singing.

Red Boots On: This text was written by the English poet Kit Wright while he was living in Canada. I love this poem; it needs to be sung with a spikey, cheeky confidence, and have a touch of Joni Mitchell or the Chenille Sisters in the sound! The piece is written for four parts, but it can be sung with only two by omitting certain lines, as detailed in the footnote on the first page.

for the ABCD North West Honour Choir, Summer 2007

All for Love of One

Anon. 15th cent.

BOB CHILCOTT

I must go walk the wood so wild And wan - der here and there

In dread and dead - ly__ fear, For where I__ trust-ed I am be - guiled.__ And

If performing in unison, sing the soprano line in bars 24–31 and the alto line in bars 31–39 and 55–63.

Commissioned by The Young Voices of Colorado for the 2008
Sing a Mile High Children's Choir Festival, Artistic Director Jena Dickey

The Truth is Great

Coventry Patmore (1823–96)

BOB CHILCOTT

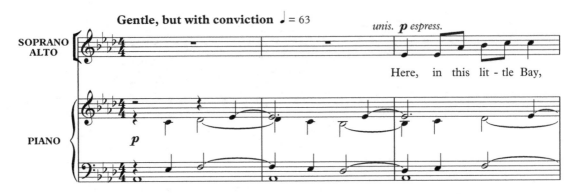

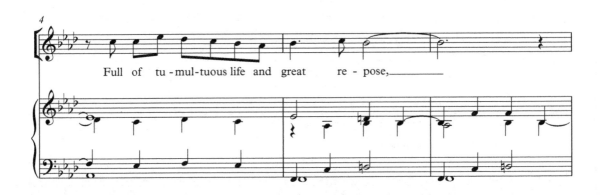

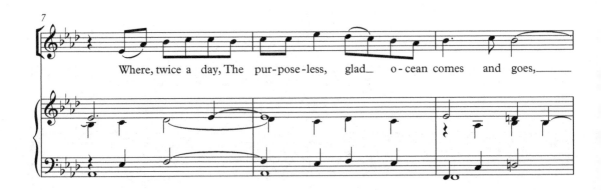

If performing in unison, omit the alto line when the parts divide.

Commissioned by The Young Voices of Colorado for the 2008
Sing a Mile High Children's Choir Festival, Artistic Director Jena Dickey

Circles of Motion

Joy Harjo (b. 1951)

BOB CHILCOTT

Cir - cled in_ blue sky, swept our hearts clean With sa - cred

wings._____

S. *mp*
A.
We see you, see our - selves and

mp sonore

p dolce
S.
know_____ That we must take the ut - most care And
A.

p dolce

p dolce

ea - gle round-ing out the morn - ing,_____ We_

S.
A.
pray it will be done_____

a tempo
unis. *dolce*
In beau - ty,_____ in beau - ty,_____

dolce

_ in beau - ty,_____ in beau - ty._

Commissioned by the Ames Children's Choirs, Founder and Conductor Sylvia Munsen,
for the Midwest Children's Choir Festival, Bob Chilcott, Guest Conductor 27 April 2007

All things pass

Lau-Tzu (6th-cent. BC)

BOB CHILCOTT

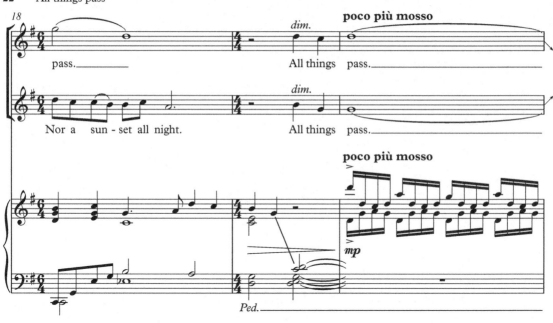

pass._____   All things   pass._____

Nor a   sun - set all night.   All things   pass._____

What al - ways   chan - ges?_____

What al - ways   chan - ges?_____   Earth,

change,   And if these do   not last,

mp *legato espress.*

and   if   these   do   not   last,

Do man's vi — sions   last?

Do man's il – lu – sions   last?

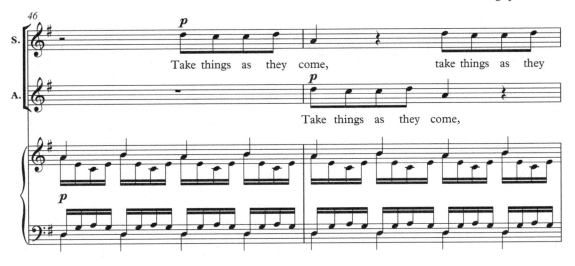

Take things as they come, take things as they

Take things as they come,

come.

take things as they come.

For the 30th Anniversary of the St Louis Children's Choirs, Artistic Director Barbara Berner.
A gift from Carna Manthey for Adrienne Broyles' Level I Children's Choir

Red Boots On

Kit Wright (b. 1944)

BOB CHILCOTT

If performing in two parts, sing the first and second soprano lines in bars 19–22 and 37–44, and the second soprano and second alto lines in bar 48–51.